Cambridge English Readers

Level 4

Series editor: Philip Prowse

High Life, Low Life

Alan Battersby

CAMBRIDGE
UNIVERSITY PRESS

CAMBRIDGE UNIVERSITY PRESS
Cambridge, New York, Melbourne, Madrid, Cape Town,
Singapore, São Paulo, Delhi, Tokyo, Mexico City

Cambridge University Press
The Edinburgh Building, Cambridge CB2 8RU, UK

www.cambridge.org
Information on this title: www.cambridge.org/9780521788151

First published 2001
12th printing 2012

Printed in China by Sheck Wah Tong Printing Press Limited

A catalogue record for this publication is available from the British Library

ISBN 978-0-521-78815-1 Paperback
ISBN 978-0-521-68608-2 Paperback plus audio CD pack

Contents

Characters

Nat Marley: New York private investigator
Stella Delgado: Nat Marley's personal assistant
Annie Clayton: a homeless woman
Mrs. Joanna Whittaker: a rich widow
Martha Bianchi: Mrs. Whittaker's maid
Charlie Whittaker: Mrs. Whittaker's son
Betty Osborne: Mrs. Whittaker's daughter
Wilma Patterson: a lawyer
Jackie Robinson Clayton: Annie Clayton's son
Ernie Wiseman (Ernst Weissmann): a criminal
Captain Oldenberg: detective with the New York Police Department (NYPD)
Joe Blaney: colleague of Nat Marley, ex-NYPD
Dr. Fischer: a doctor at Bellevue Hospital

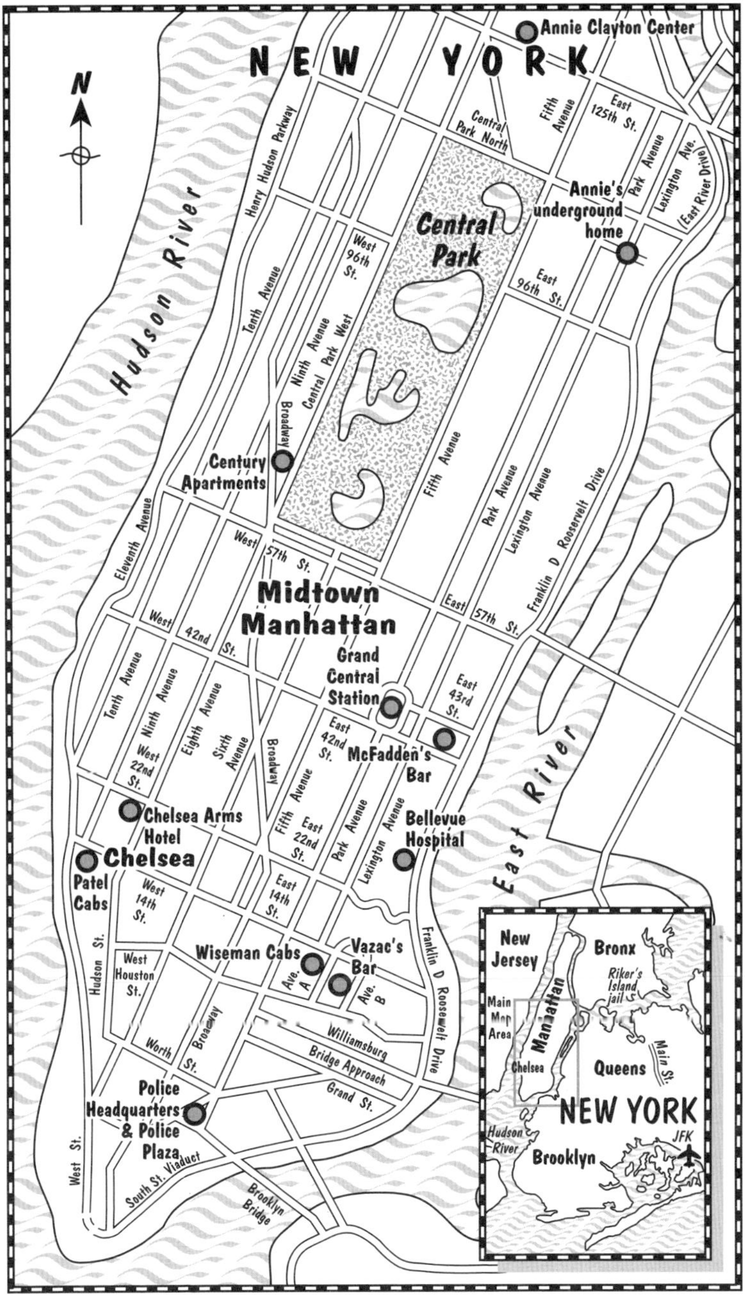
NEW YORK
N
Annie Clayton Center
Henry Hudson Parkway
Central Park North
Fifth Avenue
East 125th St.
Park Avenue
Lexington Ave.
(East River Drive)
Annie's underground home
Hudson River
Central Park
West 96th St.
East 96th St.
Tenth Avenue
Ninth Avenue
Central Park West
Broadway
Century Apartments
Fifth Avenue
Park Avenue
Lexington Avenue
Franklin D Roosevelt Drive
Eleventh Avenue
West 57th St.
Midtown Manhattan
East 57th St.
West 42nd St.
Grand Central Station
East 43rd St.
Tenth Avenue
Ninth Avenue
Eighth Avenue
Sixth Avenue
Broadway
East 42nd St.
McFadden's Bar
West 22nd St.
Fifth Avenue
East 22nd St.
Park Avenue
Lexington Avenue
Bellevue Hospital
East River
Chelsea Arms Hotel
Chelsea
Patel Cabs
West 14th St.
East 14th St.
Hudson St.
West Houston St.
Wiseman Cabs
Ave. A
Vazac's Bar
Ave. B
Franklin D Roosevelt Drive
Worth St.
Broadway
Williamsburg Bridge Approach
Grand St.
Police Headquarters & Police Plaza
West St.
South St. Viaduct
Brooklyn Bridge
New Jersey
Bronx
Riker's Island jail
Main Map Area
Manhattan
Chelsea
Queens
Main St.
NEW YORK
Hudson River
Brooklyn
JFK

Chapter 1 *Summer in the city*

They say if you don't like the heat, get out of the kitchen. New York, mid-July, if you don't like the heat, get out of the city. Anyone who could take a vacation was in the mountains or on Long Island. Anywhere cooler than the city. But me, I had work to do and dollars to earn. As I left my apartment building in Queens, the heat hit me. The temperature was already up in the eighties. Only seven o'clock in the morning and I was sweating. It was going to be another one of those hot, uncomfortable days. Time to catch the number seven train to Manhattan.

The name's Marley, Nat Marley. I know the city of New York like the back of my hand. New York is part of me, it's in my blood. During my fifteen years' service with the New York Police Department, I saw the best and worst of life in the city. After leaving the NYPD, I became a private investigator. Although I don't make that much money, I'm my own boss and I don't have to take orders from anybody. I prefer it that way.

At Grand Central Station, crowds of office workers hurried out to 42nd Street. There were usually a few homeless people in the station trying to make a few dollars before the police moved them along. When you make the same trip every day, you get to know people's faces. But today, I couldn't see any homeless people. Maybe they were out in the sunshine on 42nd Street.

Suddenly a voice called out, "Hey, Nat, don't you recognize me?"

I turned around. There was an old woman in an expensive-looking coat and skirt. It was Annie, a real New York character: one of the homeless people I'd known since I was a patrolman with the NYPD.

"Do you like my coat, Nat? I found it in the trash."

"A winter coat in July? You must be boiling. I like the coat, but you don't look too great, Annie."

"I'm OK, Nat. Anyway, a winter coat's valuable so it stays with me, sunshine or snow."

I looked at her closely. There was something different about her. I couldn't say what exactly. But she had changed.

"Sure you're feeling all right, Annie?"

"Me, Nat? Never felt better."

Maybe she was just exhausted from trying to earn a living on the streets at her age. But something told me I should stay around.

"I'll buy you breakfast. Coffee and doughnuts?" I offered.

Annie took my arm as we made our way toward the main entrance. Suddenly she pulled at my jacket.

"Hey, not so fast, Nat. Just give me a minute. It's this pain in my chest."

I looked at her closely. The sweat was pouring off her face. We hadn't walked far, but she was out of breath. She held my hand tightly. Her skin felt cold.

"Oh my God!" she cried.

She reached for her chest, her eyes and mouth wide open in pain. Then she fell at my feet, unconscious. A heart attack. I felt her wrist. There was no pulse. There was no movement from her chest either. She wasn't breathing. I didn't have time to think. All that NYPD training came back to me. First the breathing. Head back, hold the nose, open mouth, check the airway. Close my lips over the mouth. Breathe out, pause, and again. Then both hands on her chest. Push down. Again, fifteen times. I looked up at the circle of people around us.

"Someone call 911. Get an ambulance! Anyone here done first aid training?" I asked.

A guy stepped forward nervously. "I've just taken a first aid course," he said.

"Start with the breathing, then we'll change over."

We worked on her for five long minutes. I felt Annie's wrist again. This time there was a pulse. And then some movement in her chest. At last, I heard the sound of the ambulance siren.

The ambulance men took over and put Annie in the ambulance waiting on 42nd Street. I knew someone like her wouldn't have health insurance.

"You taking her to Bellevue Hospital?" I asked.

"Yeah."

"Here's my card. Any questions about hospital bills, tell them to call me."

How I would actually pay any hospital bills was another matter.

A police officer came over to interview me. As soon as he left me, a reporter from the *Daily News* ran up to me.

"Can I ask a few questions, sir? This is going to be a great story."

I didn't mind. The story might be good for business.

From Grand Central, it was five minutes' walk to my office at 220 East 43rd Street. Most offices in the building had their own air conditioning. Mine didn't, so it was hot and uncomfortable.

It was very quiet in the office when I arrived. No surprises there. Business is usually quiet in July. Even bad guys take vacations.

Stella Delgado, my personal assistant, was already at her desk. She looked tired and annoyed.

"Nat, when are we going to get air conditioning?" she asked. "It's impossible to work. And look at the sweat on your shirt!"

"I've been on my knees at Grand Central," I said, "saving an old lady's life. That's hard work in this heat."

I told Stella what had just happened. She stopped complaining about the heat.

"Let's go and see how she is," she suggested.

New York private investigators don't normally use public transportation. But I'm different. Stella and I took a number 15 bus downtown on Second Avenue then walked one block east to the hospital on First Avenue. I introduced myself to the receptionist.

"The name's Nat Marley. I'm a close friend of Annie Clayton's. She's just been admitted to the emergency room. We have to see her, miss. You see . . ."

"Sorry. Family only in the emergency room," the receptionist said.

"Look, miss. She's more like family to me than my own wife," I said.

That was true. I hadn't seen much of Mrs. Marley since the divorce.

"I'll call the emergency room and see what they say," replied the receptionist.

We were allowed to visit. Stella and I waited outside an examination room where a doctor was checking Annie's heart. Eventually the doctor came out and introduced herself.

"Mr. Marley? I'm Dr. Fischer. The rules say family only in here, but this is a special case. So you're the guy who saved Mrs. Clayton at Grand Central? You did a good job there."

"Is she going to be all right, Doctor?" I asked.

Her face told me all I needed to know. "She's a fighter, but she's had a serious heart attack," she said.

Annie was sleeping, and we waited over an hour before we were allowed in to see her. She looked exhausted but she smiled when she saw me.

"Nat, it's good to see you," she said. "And thanks."

"It was nothing, Annie. I save lives every day," I said.

"Nat, I've been thinking. I may not have much time left. This morning was no surprise. I've had heart trouble for years. Nat, can you find me a lawyer? I want to make a will."

I wondered what Annie had to leave anybody after she died. Anyway, I agreed to do as she asked. I knew an excellent family lawyer, Wilma Patterson. I called her and she agreed to come over to the hospital that afternoon.

This was the beginning of the strange story of two old ladies from the opposite ends of New York society – the high life and the low life. Two old ladies who had never met and whose lives were very different. This is the story of how those lives came together.

Chapter 2 *Central Park West*

The next morning, my picture was on an inside page of the *Daily News*, with the full story. It read "Dying Woman Saved." The story began:

"Yesterday, without the quick thinking of private investigator Nat Marley, Annie Clayton, a homeless New Yorker, would have died at Grand Central Station . . ."

Around eleven o'clock, a messenger arrived with a letter. The address was written in very careful handwriting. I had a new job title:

"To Mr. Nat Marley, Senior Investigator, the Marley Investigation Agency."

"Wow, that makes you look important, Nat!" said Stella.

The letter was from Mrs. Joanna Whittaker, Apartment 1543, Century Apartments, 25 Central Park West. That's one expensive address. The Century Apartments were the last of the fashionable apartment buildings completed before the Great Depression of the 1930s.

The letter read:

Dear Mr. Marley,

I have just read about you in the Daily News. *I would like your agency to do a special service for me. I need a professional.*

I do not leave my apartment, and I wish to speak to you in private. The doorman will be expecting you. You may call on me any afternoon between 12:00 and 1:00.

Yours truly,

Joanna Whittaker (Mrs.)

"What do you think, Stella?" I asked.

"Interesting," said Stella.

"Shall we visit the lady? We could go now – nothing's happening here."

For once, I looked smart. I had put on a clean shirt and my good jacket, which was just back from the cleaner's. Stella was wearing her new suit. We looked like complete professionals.

"Stella, we're taking a cab," I said.

"A cab! Sure you're feeling all right?" she asked in surprise.

I'd never felt better. We could be visiting several million dollars so we had to look cool and fresh. Usually, I hate spending money on cabs, but if you want to look good in July, you don't walk.

It was 11:30 and the traffic wasn't moving much quicker than you could walk. I felt sorry for the cab drivers. We drove slowly across town and up to Columbus Circle, then uptown along Central Park West to Century Apartments. One of the best addresses in Manhattan.

When we got there I gave my name to the doorman.

"Mrs. Whittaker's expecting you Mr. Marley. But I'll have to warn her first. Don't want the old lady to get too excited."

He picked up the phone. Nothing for over a minute.

"This could take some time," the doorman explained.

"She sometimes gets confused. Hello. Is this Martha? It's Bob in the lobby. I have some visitors for Mrs. Whittaker . . . Yes, Mr. Nathan Marley and his personal assistant Ms. Stella Delgado . . . Yes, I'll send them up."

Inside the elevator, it was all dark wood, thick carpets and mirrors. If this was just the elevator, imagine what the apartments were like. Would I ever live in a place like this? On my income, only in my dreams. I rang the bell of the apartment and waited. A minute later, I rang again. Eventually the door opened. A large middle-aged woman stared at me unpleasantly.

"You Mr. Marley?" she asked.

"Yes, ma'am. With my assistant Ms. Stella Delgado."

"Show me your license."

I passed her my private investigator's license.

"Just a minute," she said and shut the door in my face.

Another wait. She returned, and without a word showed us in to the living room where an old lady was waiting.

"Mr. Marley and Miss Delgado, how do you do? I'm Joanna Whittaker. Do sit down. Martha, tea for our guests."

I looked around the room which was full of beautiful 1940s furniture. Nothing had been changed for years and I felt like I was in an old Hollywood movie. I wondered who would walk in next – Cary Grant or Joan Crawford?

Martha returned with cups and two teapots. She didn't exactly look pleased to receive visitors. Her thick, strong arms held the heavy tea things with no effort at all.

"Assam or Darjeeling tea, Mr. Marley?" asked Mrs. Whittaker.

I wasn't sure of the difference, but I wasn't about to

admit that.

"Assam, thank you, ma'am. Three sugars."

"Oh good! I like a man with a sweet tooth. Just like my poor husband used to have. And you, Miss Delgado?"

"Darjeeling, please," Stella replied.

"My husband took this place when we were married," said Mrs. Whittaker. "I've lived here ever since. At one time, this apartment was full of laughter and happiness. But since my poor husband died there's just been myself and Martha. Martha does everything for me – I never leave the apartment. She's been with the family for years. She's almost part of the furniture."

There was a sound of glass breaking in the kitchen. Mrs. Whittaker didn't hear it. Someone didn't like being called part of the furniture.

"Do you have any family?" asked Stella.

"A son and a daughter. They don't live in the city. Charlie's in Albany and Betty's in Syracuse. I'd like to see more of them. Especially the grandchildren, but . . ."

The old lady's eyes filled with tears. Stella took her hand. She knew exactly what to do. I'm no good in situations like these.

"Now don't cry, ma'am. We understand," said Stella.

"Do you? . . . I'm sorry, Miss."

"No need to apologize," I said.

"Thank you. I'm all right," she said. Then she looked at me. "Now, Tom," she said, "let's get down to business."

"Tom?" I asked, looking back at her.

"Did I say Tom?" she asked. "Oh, silly me! My mistake. You know, you look so much like my poor dead husband. Now where was I? Oh, yes, Mr. Marley, I need a lawyer."

Chapter 3 *The will*

"Mrs. Whittaker," I said, "I'm not a lawyer."

"I may be old, but I'm not completely stupid," the old lady replied. "I want you to *find* me a lawyer."

"Where's the phone book?" I asked. "I'll show you who to call."

"You don't understand. I want you to find a good lawyer and bring him here. Someone I can trust. It's to do with my will."

Mrs. Whittaker opened her handbag and took out a pile of hundred-dollar bills. I hadn't seen so much money in one place in years.

"What's your fee, Mr. Marley?"

"It's one thousand dollars a day plus expenses. But not just now, ma'am. When I finish the job. I wouldn't carry all that money around. It could be dangerous."

We left the coolness of the lobby at the Century Apartments and walked out onto Central Park West. If you don't like the heat, find a bar. Which is what we did. A short walk through the park to the Tavern on the Green. Not the sort of place I would choose to drink in. Expensive drinks and too many tourists. But it was close. That's important when it's hot enough to fry an egg on the sidewalk.

We sat in a quiet corner with a couple of cold beers and talked about the two women we had just met.

"What a way to live!" said Stella.

"Yeah. Can you imagine it? Never going outside," I replied. "As far as I can see, Martha does everything for Mrs. Whittaker. She looks as if she's got the strength. Strange woman, though. I wouldn't want to meet Martha on a dark lonely street."

Stella remained silent. I could see she was thinking.

"There's something very strange about Mrs. Whittaker, too," she said finally. "She's got family, so why doesn't she have her own family lawyer? And I couldn't see any photos of her children. Just wedding photos and pictures of her husband. Then she called you 'Tom.' Who does she think you are? Her husband returned from the dead?"

"Who knows what's going on!" I said. "But worrying about it isn't going to earn us any money. Let's go and find that lawyer."

Stella and I went back to the office and I made a call to Wilma Patterson. By three o'clock we had made the arrangements. We met Wilma back at the Century Apartments and took the elevator up to the fifteenth floor. Martha showed us in without a word.

"Ah, Mr. Marley and Miss Delgado. But where is my lawyer?" asked Mrs. Whittaker.

Wilma stopped her. "Mrs. Whittaker, I am Wilma Patterson, senior partner of Patterson and Schofield, attorneys-at-law."

"I don't believe you!" Mrs. Whittaker said sharply.

"Mrs. Whittaker," I said, "Mrs. Patterson is the finest lawyer I know. Trust me."

Mrs. Whittaker looked at me doubtfully. I just nodded and smiled. Eventually she relaxed.

"Well, well. These modern times. I wasn't expecting a

lady lawyer. Now do sit down. You will join me in a glass of sherry, won't you? Martha!"

Martha came in with bottles and glasses. She looked angry. Mrs. Whittaker waved her away to the kitchen without so much as a "thank you."

"Sweet or dry, Mr. Marley?" she asked.

I don't drink sherry, but I didn't want to upset Mrs. Whittaker. I asked for sweet.

"A very good choice, Tom," she said, smiling. "Oh dear! There I go again, calling you Tom. Now Tom always enjoyed a sweet sherry. And you do too. Now Mr. Marley, if you would wait here with Miss Delgado. I have business to discuss with Mrs. Patterson in the library."

I knew this was going to take time. I made myself comfortable and had a couple more sherries. After a while, Stella fell asleep. I started putting prices on the furniture in the living room and lost count at $50,000.

An hour later, Wilma returned, looking worried. "Nat, we have a problem," she said. "Mrs. Whittaker wants to make you rich."

"Is that a problem?" I asked.

"It is when the son and daughter don't get a cent. I've talked it over with her, but she won't listen. She wants it all to go to you. She read about you in the papers. Says you remind her of her late husband, Tom. Says she couldn't think of a better person to leave everything to."

The door to the kitchen was open. Suddenly there was the sound of more glass breaking. Did Martha have a lot of accidents, or was she listening to every word that was being said and didn't like what she heard?

"So what happens now?" I asked.

"In the end, I don't have much choice," said Wilma. "A lawyer has to follow the client's instructions."

"I don't like this," I said. "You've got to speak to the family and arrange a meeting. Or else I'm going to be in the middle of a family war."

"Agreed," she replied. "But I'm not making any promises."

Wilma went back in the library. Then I heard the sound of someone using an old typewriter. A couple more sherries later, I was starting to get a headache. I got up and looked more closely at one of the photos of Tom Whittaker. Forty-something, a little fat, and losing his hair. Just like me, unfortunately. The sound of typing went on. At five o'clock, Wilma came out to ask Stella to sign the will as a witness and the doorman was called from downstairs to be the second witness. A few minutes later, everybody was back in the sitting room. Mrs. Whittaker looked pleased.

"Thank you, everybody," Mrs. Whittaker said. "Mr. Marley, your fee."

She gave me a fat envelope.

"Mrs. Patterson has already given me her bill." Mrs. Whittaker gave Wilma another fat envelope.

"Now, before you leave, a present for everybody. Martha . . . *Martha*!"

Martha entered with a pile of large books in her powerful arms.

"In memory of my dear husband," said Mrs. Whittaker.

I looked at the title: *A History of Whittaker Air* by Tom Whittaker, President. So that was where the family money came from.

"Thank you so much, ma'am. I'll enjoy reading this," I lied.

Mrs. Whittaker gave me a big sweet smile. Almost like she was in love. It frightened me. She took my hand. Her hand was all bone and paper-thin skin. At that point, I just wanted get out of that apartment and never return.

"You'll enjoy living here when I'm gone, Tom," she said.

Martha was standing behind everybody. She gave Mrs. Whittaker a long dark look.

Finally we escaped into the late afternoon heat. Outside, I opened the envelope; two thousand dollars in hundred-dollar bills. Not bad for one day's work.

Wilma Patterson looked worried.

"Nat, once the family finds out about the will, there's going to be trouble," she said.

"Don't I know it!" I replied. "You've got to get the family talking. Get her to change the will."

"As I said before, I'll try," Wilma replied.

"Thanks," I said. "I don't want anyone to think I take advantage of confused old ladies."

Chapter 4 *Beneath the city streets*

By the time we got back to East 43rd Street, it was past six o'clock. No point trying to do any work. I wandered over to McFadden's Bar on Second Avenue. The usual crowd of *Daily News* reporters was there, doing what they did best – drinking.

I needed information and I knew just the guy who could help – Ed Winchester. He used to be the crime reporter at the *Daily News*, and he still did some part-time work. Once a reporter, always a reporter.

"Nat, my old friend!" Ed said when he saw me. "You've arrived at just the right moment."

"Does that mean your glass is empty, Ed?" I asked, and waved to the bartender. "Jack! Sam Adams for me and a drink for Ed."

It was time for Ed to earn his drink. I told him about our strange meeting with Mrs. Whittaker and the business of the will. I asked what he knew about the family. I knew I could depend on Ed – he had a very long memory.

Ed took a drink and said, "Hmm . . . Tom Whittaker. Now, he's the guy who started one of the first regular air services between New York and Chicago in the 1920s. The business became very successful in the 1950s and 1960s. Then he sold it. I think it became part of Pan Am. I'll see what else I can find out."

"So the family's got money?" I asked.

"Lots of it," Ed said.

It had been a long day and I was getting a headache. I left and took the number seven train home to Queens. I couldn't eat much of the takeout meal I got from the diner down the block. That night, I lay awake for hours. It was dawn before I finally fell asleep. In the morning, I didn't feel very active. I went off to work like a machine. Not a thought or an idea in my head. Take my advice – avoid New York in July.

When I arrived at the office, Stella was already at work. Inside, it didn't feel as hot as usual. There were two electric fans on her desk. I could see through the door to my office. Another two fans.

"Morning, Stella. Where did those fans come from?" I asked.

"Macy's," she replied. "I phoned yesterday. They were the last ones in the store. We were lucky to get them. Here's the bill."

"What's this?" I asked. "Two hundred dollars! Do you think I'm made of money?"

"I can't work if I don't have the fans," said Stella. "If I can't work, I don't make you any money. It's as simple as that."

I was about to argue when the phone rang. It was Dr. Fischer at Bellevue Hospital. Annie was asking to see me. Apparently, it was important.

When I got to Annie's room, she was sitting up in bed, but she looked awful. There was a visitor with her.

"Nat, it's good to see you," Annie said weakly. "This is Leona, an old friend. Leona, meet Nat. He's going to help me with some family business. And before you ask, Nat, I'll pay you somehow."

"I wouldn't dream of asking for money, Annie," I said. I was there to help out an old friend. Annie was already sick enough without knowing what my daily fee was.

"A man can't put food on the table by working for nothing," Annie said. "Nat, I want you to go with Leona. She's going to take you somewhere you've never been before."

In my fifteen years' service with the NYPD, I'd been to most places in New York City. I wondered where Leona was going to take me. We left the hospital and walked four blocks west to the subway station on 28th Street. Then we took an uptown number six train to 103rd Street and Lexington. Some New Yorkers never go further uptown than 96th Street on the East Side. For them, anywhere north is like a foreign country. At 103rd Street, it does feel like another world. There are no expensive stores, good restaurants, or skyscrapers. The only tall buildings are the housing projects, low cost apartments built for working people. The people on the streets are mostly African-American and Latino.

"So what's new, Leona?" I asked. "I used to walk these streets when I was a patrolman."

"Just be patient, Nat," she replied. "You ain't seen nothing yet."

Leona took me across Lexington to an old building. It looked empty. But the door opened as soon as Leona knocked. A big man welcomed Leona, but then looked at me with a cold stare, pointed, and asked, "What's this guy doing here?"

"He's OK," explained Leona. "He's cool. Nat's doing a little job for Annie."

Leona took me down some steps. At the bottom there was a hole in the wall and she led me through it. I could hardly see my hand in front of my face.

"Where are we, Leona?" I asked.

"Below the streets. This is the city you don't know. Careful now, there's a train coming."

A downtown number five train passed. The light from the train windows helped me see where we were – the subway. There were four train tracks, two uptown and two downtown and a narrow path beside the tracks. Ahead of us was a subway station, but no lights.

"Welcome to our home, Nat," Leona said. "This station isn't used any more, so we moved in."

I'd heard of people living underground in New York, but I'd never seen it for myself. I could see a light ahead. "Home" was an old, wooden change booth, the type I remember from my childhood. A woman was sitting in an armchair by the door.

"Ellie, this guy's a friend. He's helping Annie with some family business. I'll put some coffee on."

"You know what?" I said, looking around. "You've got a nice place down here. Better than my place in Queens. You live down here all the time?" I asked.

"Sure we do," replied Ellie. "Cool in the summer and we manage to keep warm in the winter. And we don't pay rent."

"Are you safe down here?"

"We've lived on the streets," Leona said. "I can tell you, it's safer underground. Everyone knows each other here. If a stranger comes, we know about it. The subway workers know us. They leave us alone."

Leona started moving piles of black plastic bags. Underneath was an old metal box with a lock.

"Nat," she said, "Annie wants you to take this box to her."

Leona took me back up to the street. As I traveled back downtown to 28th Street, I wondered how many more underground communities I was passing on the subway.

Back at the hospital, I gave Annie the box. Then she took out a key that was tied around her neck, unlocked the box, and showed me a photograph of a cheerful teenage boy.

"Nat," said Annie, "this is my son, Jackie. I haven't seen him in twenty years. I want you to find him."

"I never knew you had family," I said.

"You don't know everything about me. I may not have long to live, Nat, and I want to see him again before I die. We lived in a housing project in the South Bronx. Not a nice area. After leaving home, Jackie used to visit now and then. Usually to borrow money. I knew he wasn't a good kid, but he's my son. His father was the top man in an office where I once worked as a cleaner. The sort of guy who tells every woman his wife doesn't understand him. I was lonely and we had a good time. He made me laugh, and Jackie's the result."

"How old is he now?" I asked.

"Born in 1954, so about your age," Annie said. "I last saw him in Riker's Island jail in 1979. He'd been stealing cars and getting into fights. It's easy to find the wrong type of friends in the Bronx. When I visited him in jail, he said he never wanted to see me again. It broke my heart. From that point, my life went to pieces. I was feeling really low and that's when I started living on the streets of Manhattan. I had to escape, get out of the Bronx, and forget."

"Anything else you can tell me?" I asked.

"I once heard he was living on the Lower East Side," she said. "Working as a cab driver."

"A cab driver, you say? If he had a police record he couldn't get a job as a cab driver. His full name?"

"Jackie Robinson Clayton."

"Height?" I asked.

"About five feet ten inches," Annie said weakly. "Oh, and he's got a tattoo of a bird, the American eagle, on his left arm. When you find him, tell him his mother wants to see him. Bring him here. It's important."

"I'll do my best, Annie," I said, "but don't raise your hopes too much. This could be a difficult one."

Annie gave me the photo and locked the box. Then she asked me to take the box and key to Wilma Patterson's office. She lay back on the bed, sweating and breathing heavily. I called the nurse. Annie looked more dead than alive.

Chapter 5 *Inside information*

I got to McFadden's Bar at lunch time. Inside, it was noisy and busy, but cool, thanks to the air conditioning. I realized I was hungry. I hadn't eaten properly since breakfast the day before. I ordered a steak with extra fries. As I was eating, Jack, the bartender, called me.

"Hey, Nat, there's a guy here says you're buying him a drink." I looked up. Ed Winchester was waving an empty glass.

"Well, I guess I am," I said. "Over here, Ed. And this had better be good."

"I like doing business this way," said Ed. "You buy me drinks and I find you information."

Ed told me he'd been in the *Daily News* library, reading up about Whittaker Air. It was a good story. Tom Whittaker was an interesting guy. He had been a U.S. Air Service pilot and was shot down in France in the First World War. He was one of the lucky few who made it home. When he got out of the air service, he bought a couple of ex-air service planes and started flying people around the city. Sightseeing by air. In the late 1920s he started an airline business. Flights to Washington and Chicago. He saw that the future was air travel. During the 1950s the railroads were beginning to lose passengers to the airlines and Whittaker Air was taking a big share of them.

"Was he the sort of guy who lived for his work?" I asked.

"Not at all," replied Ed. "He was quite a ladies' man. Look at this: *Daily News*, 1957."

Ed gave me a photocopy of a newspaper story. There was Tom Whittaker at a table in a cocktail bar with three amazing-looking blondes. Each one better built and better looking than Marilyn Monroe. Whittaker looked pleased with himself. I could understand why.

"Just look at him," said Ed. "He could be your brother."

"We might look alike," I said, "but he had everything I don't have. Money and women."

Ed went on to tell me that Tom Whittaker worked hard and played hard. Even after he was married he played around with other women. It wasn't a happy marriage and he and Mrs. Whittaker probably stayed together for the children. He sold Whittaker Air to Pan Am in the late 1960s. Then he spent most of his time on City Island, drinking and fishing. He died in 1974.

"Goodbye, Tom Whittaker," I said.

"You're in luck, buddy," said Ed. "When she dies, you can afford drinks for everyone."

I walked back to East 43rd Street. Stella was busy at the computer when I arrived at the office.

"Hi, Stella," I said. "I've just been speaking to Ed."

"Don't you mean speaking and drinking?" Stella replied.

"Yeah. With Ed you can't do one without the other."

I told Stella everything I'd learned from Ed.

"You know, Nat, it frightens me – Mrs. Whittaker, Martha, that apartment," she said.

"Uh-huh. Like something out of a horror movie."

"You said it," Stella added. "And imagine never going out. What sort of life is that? Mrs. Whittaker's not right in the head."

"She isn't if she's left money to me," I said. "Any clients for me to see?"

"The phone hasn't rung all day," said Stella.

"Oh well. I'm going to Century Apartments to see the one person I know there who's not crazy. Bob the doorman."

I arrived at Century Apartments and walked into the lobby. The air conditioning was working perfectly. It was like walking into December.

"Bob, remember me?" I asked.

"Ah, Mr. Marley," he said.

"Call me Nat. I'd like to ask you a few questions about Mrs. Whittaker."

"Now, Mr. Marley . . . Nat," he said. "I really shouldn't talk about our . . ."

"Would this help?" I asked.

I showed him my investigator's license. That helped a little. I also showed him a fifty-dollar bill. That helped a lot.

"Why, thank you," he said.

"How does Mrs. Whittaker get everything she needs?" I asked.

"Martha does some of the shopping, or the stores send things to the apartment. Mrs. Whittaker is the type of lady who likes to be looked after."

"Does she get many visitors?"

"I've been here five years," Bob said. "In that time, the

only visitors I've seen are her son and daughter. Even they've only been here three or four times. The last time I saw them was over two years ago. I remember because they were both angry when they left. The daughter was in tears. Family disagreement or something."

So Mrs. Whittaker saw nobody except for Martha, I thought. Not a healthy way of life.

Chapter 6 *East Village*

Now and then the elevator breaks down at the office. This was one of those days. After walking up eight floors, I felt hot and uncomfortable. The fans didn't make much difference. Fall couldn't come soon enough.

I had phone calls to make. At last, real work – finding a missing person – Annie's son, Jackie. My first call was to Police Headquarters. I knew someone who could help, someone I used to work with. That is, if he wasn't feeling too bad tempered.

"Get me Captain Oldenberg, will you?"

"Marley!" Oldenberg shouted, "I've got enough problems without you calling me."

"You don't sound happy in your work," I said. "Listen, I'm trying to find a missing person, a Jackie Robinson Clayton. He's been in trouble. He was in Riker's Island in 1979. He may be working as a cab driver now. Forty-six years old, medium height, the American eagle on his left arm."

"Anything else?" Oldenberg asked.

"Nothing," I said. "His mother hasn't seen him in twenty years. And Oldenberg, this is a job for an old friend."

"OK, Marley," said Oldenberg. "But I'm not lifting a finger in this heat. I'll get Lieutenant Brandstein to do it."

"First thing," I said, "get him to check if the guy's in prison, will you?"

Next I needed some information from the *Daily News*. I put a call through to Ed Winchester. Luckily, he was back from McFadden's Bar.

"Nat, what can I do for you?" he asked

"I'm trying to find a guy by the name of Jackie Robinson Clayton," I said. "He's been in trouble, so there might be some news stories on him."

I gave Ed the information he needed. I crossed my fingers and hoped he would turn up something.

The phone rang as soon as I put it down. Lieutenant Brandstein was doing a good job. Jackie Clayton was not in jail anywhere in the U.S.A. We were doing well. I was beginning to enjoy myself. This was what life as a private investigator should be like. I even forgot how hot it was. Now I needed some extra help. Joe Blaney was just the guy. He was a big tough ex-cop who did work for me sometimes.

"Joe, it's Nat. Listen, my life is full of old ladies at the moment. I've got a strange client – a Mrs. Joanna Whittaker. And Martha, who lives with her, is even stranger. I need to know more about them." I gave Joe the story so far with the address and descriptions.

"Boss," Joe said, "You sure do meet some crazy people."

I spent the next morning looking around the Lower East Side, trying to find Jackie. Often, when you turn over a stone, you find something unpleasant beneath it. It can be the same with families. The more you find out, the more dirt you discover. I was hoping this wasn't going to happen with Jackie.

No luck at any of the cab companies or bars I visited. How far could you get looking for a guy in his mid-forties using a photo of him as a teenager? Finally, I found a cab driver on Canal Street in Chinatown who'd heard of Jackie. He told me to try the East Village.

I started on Avenues A, B and C, once known as Alphabet City. It was a total waste of time until I got to Vazac's Bar on Avenue B.

I showed the bartender Jackie's picture. When I told him about the tattoo, I could see he'd heard of him. He gave me a dark look.

"You a cop or something?" he asked.

"No, buddy," I said. "The name's Marley. Just an honest private investigator."

I showed him my license.

"I don't talk to cops or private eyes, mister," the bartender said.

"Nice friendly place you got here. A guy could feel very welcome. Do you talk to money?"

I turned my license round. Behind it was a twenty-dollar bill. As the bartender reached for it, I pulled my hand away.

"Not so fast. What've you got?" I asked.

"OK, I know him," he said. "Haven't seen him recently. He's got money, but it doesn't come from driving a cab."

"Oh yeah?" I said. "So where does it all come from?"

"Buying what people steal," he replied. "If you got something hot, go to Jackie. Don't make him angry though – he's tough."

"Do you know who he works for?" I asked.

"Do I get my twenty bucks now?"

"Tell me who he works for," I said.

"Try Wiseman Cabs on Avenue A," said the bartender. "Just uptown from Tompkins Square Park."

I dropped the twenty-dollar bill onto the bar and walked out. I knew Tompkins Square Park well. When I was a patrolman, the park had been home to most of the homeless of the East Village. They used to call the community "Tent City." Later, they were moved on, but not without a fight, and the place was cleaned up. I found the cab office. There were a couple of cabs parked outside. I pretended to be a tourist. The guy at the desk gave me a poisonous look.

"Can you help me, mister?" I asked. "I'm on vacation. First visit to the Big Apple. I want to hire a cab for the day so I can do some real sightseeing."

The guy behind the desk looked as if he hadn't slept, washed, or shaved for days. He smelled even worse than me. He lit a cigarette then coughed for a full fifteen seconds. Finally, he was able to speak.

"Mister, we don't hire cabs out for the day," he said.

"Hey," I said. "Is this a cab company or what?"

"I repeat, we don't do it. You stupid or something?"

One thing was clear. Wiseman Cabs didn't want customers. Certainly not the sort of customers who wanted to hire cabs. They were in another line of business and I wanted to know what. I decided to surprise him.

"Mr. Wiseman?" I said.

"How do you know my name?"

"Could be something to do with the sign outside," I replied and then continued, "I'm looking for Jackie Clayton."

"Oh yeah?" he said. "What do you want with him?"

"It's private. Family business," I said.

"Well it just so happens I'm looking for him too, and

when I find him I'll . . ." He stopped as if he had said more than he had intended.

"You'll do what?" I asked.

"Get out of here!" Wiseman shouted. "I don't know why I'm talking to you. Don't stick your big nose in here again!"

I got the feeling I wasn't welcome any more. I left and called Joe Blaney on my cell phone.

"Nat here. What sort of morning have you had, Joe?"

"Great. Just had coffee and cake with Mrs. Whittaker."

"How did you manage that, Joe?"

"Easy. I know a guy who runs a flower shop on East 28th. I bought some flowers and wrote a note saying 'From your special friend Nat Marley.' Then I borrowed his shop coat and pretended I was the guy from the flower shop. That way I got up to the apartment. As soon as I said the flowers were from Mr. Marley, the old lady never stopped talking. She thinks you're wonderful."

"I know," I said. "It's troubling, isn't it?"

"Then I got Mrs. Whittaker talking about her family. She thinks the world of her late husband. I tried to get her to talk about the children, but she just said that they won't visit any more. I got her son's phone numbers from the address book on the hall table. Easy."

"That's good work, Joe. Now, I've got another job. I want you to watch Wiseman Cabs on Avenue A. Jackie used to work for them. There's something strange going on. They wouldn't let me hire a cab, so I want to know how they make their money. And get some photos."

Joe had given me work and home numbers for Charlie Whittaker. Maybe Wilma Patterson could get the Whittaker family talking. I called her office with the phone numbers. It was early evening before she got back to me.

"Nat? Wilma here. I managed to talk to Charlie Whittaker. He said they used to bring his children to visit until it got too painful. It was the way Mrs. Whittaker kept talking about her late husband, as if he were some kind of god. The truth of the matter is that it was a loveless marriage. Tom never had time for his children. In fact, Charlie says he was like a stranger to them."

"What a way to grow up," I said.

"Charlie Whittaker's agreed to try and set up a family meeting," Wilma continued. "His mother refuses to talk to him over the phone, so he'll have to visit. All this will take time. And will she agree? It's doubtful."

"Well, this is a fine mess!" I said.

"Don't blame yourself, Nat."

Chapter 7 *Developments*

It had been a long day. It was almost time for a cold beer. Stella was reading at her desk.

"How are things, Stella?" I asked.

"Everything's fine except that the office is too hot," Stella replied. "I can't work and I've got a headache."

"Message received. So everything's normal," I said. "That's what I like to hear. What are you reading about?"

"Air-conditioning units. You know what they are – smart machines that cool down rooms." She held a picture of one up.

"Dream on! These things cost money," I said.

The phone rang. It was Joe.

"Nat? I've been watching Wiseman Cabs all afternoon. There's a lot of movement in and out of that office. Cab drivers going in carrying one suitcase then coming out with a different one, and driving away. Seem to be doing everything except carrying passengers."

"Interesting. I wonder what Wiseman's up to?"

"The answer's in those suitcases, boss."

"Did you get some photos?" I asked.

"Used a whole roll of film. It's being developed now," Joe replied.

"Well done. There'll be a cold beer with your name on it waiting at McFadden's."

Why pay for a sauna when all you have to do is sit and sweat in your office? Maybe Stella was right. She was usually right about a lot of things. I was just thinking about the cold beers when Dr. Fischer phoned from Bellevue Hospital. Annie's condition was getting much worse.

"How much longer has she got, Doctor?" I asked.

"She's had heart trouble for years, and then with that heart attack at the station . . . I'm seriously worried, Mr. Marley."

"Is she still conscious?"

"Yes, but only just."

"Well, I've got something that should make her hold on," I said. "We're looking for her son and getting closer. We've found his old boss in the East Village. There seems to have been some argument between them. My guess is Jackie's keeping away from him. Just tell her we're getting close."

I felt both sad and angry as I put down the phone. Sad for the people who had to live out their lives on the streets. Angry about the society that put them on the streets.

Stella stopped reading and looked up.

"What's the matter, Nat?"

"It's Annie. If we don't find Jackie soon, she's going to die without seeing him," I said.

"Nat, I got an idea."

"Yeah?"

"Why don't I phone every cab company in the book? I could say I'm Jackie's ex-girlfriend wanting to see him again, to talk things over," Stella said.

"Good thinking. But first, I need some food and beer. I'll see you in McFadden's after you've locked up."

Ed Winchester from the *Daily News* was watching me as I finished my first beer. It was cool and delicious and hardly touched the sides of my throat as it went down. I immediately felt better.

"Nat, what a thirst! Now, have I got something for you. From the *Daily News*, five years ago. But first . . ."

"I get it. The story's going to cost me another drink. This had better be good."

Ed handed me a photocopy of a news story. The headline read "Weissmann and Clayton Not Guilty." I continued reading. "Ernst Weissmann and Jackie Clayton walked free today after being found not guilty of buying and selling stolen property."

"That's it," I said. "Joe spent the afternoon watching what was going on at Wiseman Cabs. Jackie Clayton used to work for Wiseman Cabs. In this story, Jackie was with a guy called Weissmann. Maybe he changed his name to make it sound more American."

Joe had arrived with the photos. Picture after picture of cab drivers going in and out of the office with different suitcases. And a beautiful picture of Wiseman.

"That's him," I said. "Now if we compare him with the picture of Ernst Weissmann in the *Daily News* story. Yeah, it's the same guy. And he doesn't get any prettier with age. This is NYPD work. Excuse me while I phone Captain Oldenberg."

Oldenberg was in a bad mood. He sounded as if he was about to explode. That was normal and natural. I only got worried when he was in a good mood.

"What do you want, Marley? Don't waste my time."

"Oldenberg, you remember a guy by the name of Weissmann? He was found not guilty about five years ago."

"Yeah. I'd love to get my hands on him again."

"Your dreams may come true. Get some of your boys to watch Wiseman Cabs on Avenue A. I think Weissmann, or Wiseman as he's known now, is still in the same kind of work, with the cab business as a cover."

"This sounds promising, Marley."

"And if you get Weissmann give him a hard time."

"Trust me, Marley. What have you got against him?" Oldenberg asked.

"He refused to let me hire a cab."

I knew from my time with the NYPD that Oldenberg was one of the most unpleasant people I'd ever meet. The strange thing was that I liked the guy. As long as you stayed on the right side of him, things were all right.

There was a beer waiting for me at the bar. I always have close relationships with beers.

"How's Oldenberg?" asked Joe.

"He's in a terrible mood," I answered.

"So what's new?"

Stella arrived and had brought another magazine about air conditioning. She showed me the front cover. It read: "You too can be cool, fresh, and relaxed in July. Say goodbye to the summertime blues with Antarctic Air Conditioning. Two units for under seven hundred dollars."

Under seven hundred dollars? The price was six hundred and ninety-nine. That made my temperature rise. But I knew I had lost. If it would keep Stella happy, it was well worth it.

"That's it! You win, Stella. Do it before I change my mind," I said.

"What's going on, boss?" asked Joe.

"Nat has kindly agreed to get air conditioning for the office," said Stella.

I was going to be seven hundred dollars poorer. That made me feel very sad indeed. Like when you lose a close friend. It looked like I was going to spend Mrs. Whittaker's two thousand dollars before it even reached my bank account.

Chapter 8 *A death in the family*

That night I tried to get some sleep. I remembered an idea I'd heard. Take an electric fan. Fill a bowl with plenty of ice. Put the fan behind the bowl. Turn on the fan and wait for cool air. That's what's supposed to happen. It was a small improvement until the ice turned to water. That didn't take long and I didn't have any more ice. Another sleepless night. I gave up at 3:00 AM. I could stay home and feel exhausted or go into the office and feel exhausted. At least it would be cooler traveling to work in the middle of the night.

The New York subway never stops working. And since the Mayor cleaned up the city, it's a lot safer. I didn't worry about using it at this time. At 4:00 AM, midtown Manhattan feels like another city. There's almost no-one on the streets. Even the air smells fresh. At the office, I opened the windows and turned on all the fans. Finally, I got some sleep. Stella found me there, still asleep at 8:00 AM.

"Nat!" she shouted. "Have you been drinking?"

"Honest, Stella," I said sleepily, "I couldn't sleep at home. I suppose you slept well?"

"I always do. Go out and get yourself some breakfast, Nat. And bring me back a coffee, will you?"

Outside, I could already feel the heat rising from the sidewalks. I was back in twenty minutes with coffee and doughnuts. The walk didn't do me much good. Now Stella had all four electric fans going in her office.

"Hey! Don't I even get a fan now?" I asked.

"Take them, Nat," Stella said. "I just borrow your two fans when you're out. There's a message from Dr. Fischer about Annie. No change from last night."

"She's a fighter," I said. "She's holding on for Jackie."

The phone rang. I didn't recognize the voice.

"Mr. Marley? This is Miss Bianchi at Century Apartments. You know me as Martha. The woman who takes the orders. Well, there ain't going to be no orders to take now. The old lady's dead."

"Oh?" I said. "You all right, Martha?"

"Of course I'm all right," she said. "But she ain't. She's cold."

"I'll be right there," I told her.

Things were moving too quickly for my liking. I turned to Stella. "Mrs. Whittaker has died. Close the office and let's get over there."

At Century Apartments, Bob the doorman was as surprised as I had been. It was the first he had heard about Mrs. Whittaker's death. He phoned up to the apartment. Two minutes later we were at the door. This time we got in quickly. Then, another surprise; Martha was smiling.

"Tell me what happened?" I asked.

"Sure," Martha said. "I went in with Mrs. Whittaker's morning tea, and there she was. Cold and dead. Come and take a look."

"I'll stay here," said Stella, with her hand to her mouth.

Mrs. Whittaker was in her bed. Her mouth and eyes were wide open and her skin was gray. She was very dead.

"Feel her," said Martha, lifting Mrs. Whittaker's thin arm. "She's cold."

"I'll take your word for it, Martha. And don't touch the body again. Has the doctor already seen her?"

"Why should he? Not much he can do for her now."

"What? Call the doctor now!"

While Martha was out of the room making the call, I had a quick look around. There was a bottle of pills on the bedside table. To help her sleep? I'd check on that. Everything else seemed to be completely normal. I had Charlie Whittaker's number and asked Stella to phone him with the news. She would be better at doing it than I would.

I needed to ask Martha a few questions before the doctor arrived. I found her in the kitchen with her large feet up on the table. She was reading an old detective story and listening to country music on the radio. I turned it off.

"Hey! What did you do that for?" she asked.

"Martha," I said. "We've got to talk."

"What about?"

"What do you think? Mrs. Whittaker, of course. When did you last see Mrs. Whittaker alive?" I asked.

"When I took in her hot chocolate," Martha said. "Ten o'clock last night."

"Do you normally give Mrs. Whittaker her pills?"

"Sure I do. Two at bedtime to help her sleep," Martha replied.

"And was last night like every other night?" I asked.

"Yeah, why shouldn't it be?" she said. "Why are you asking me all these questions?"

"It's my job. When did you find her this morning?"

"Same time as usual," Martha replied.

"Yes," I said patiently, "but what time is that?"

"Eight fifteen. There she was. Cold."

I looked around the kitchen. "You haven't touched anything in her room?"

"No sir," said Martha, waving her book at me. "I know that from detective stories. Never touch a thing."

But she had. The hot chocolate cup had been washed. I knew something was wrong. Martha was cheerful. She seemed to be enjoying every moment. The doctor had arrived before I could worry any more. Stella showed him in.

"Nat, this is Dr. Hughes," she said.

"Pleased to meet you," I said. "The name's Marley. I'm working for Mrs. Whittaker. Martha called me with the news."

The doctor went into the bedroom and did an examination to establish how Mrs. Whittaker had died. After a few minutes, I knocked on the door and joined him in the bedroom. The doctor had covered her with a sheet.

"To be honest, Mr. Marley, I've been expecting this," the doctor said. "She's had a heart condition for some time. A natural death. I'll make out a death certificate now. Has the family been told yet?"

"I've just been talking to the son," replied Stella. "Charlie Whittaker's on his way."

"Good. Now the body must be moved to a funeral home as quickly as possible. Obviously the family will make those arrangements," said Dr. Hughes.

I felt uncomfortable about the whole situation. Something wasn't right, but I couldn't say exactly what. Martha was standing close, listening to every word. I had to get rid of her for a while.

"Martha, coffee for everybody. And I always have chocolate chip cookies with my morning coffee," I said.

"We don't have them," said Martha.

"Here's five dollars. Go and get some, will you?"

Dr. Hughes and Stella looked surprised as Martha left.

"That should take her ten minutes," I said.

"Nat, why are you sending Martha shopping?" asked Stella.

"Martha's far too cheerful for my liking," I said. "And I don't want her listening in to every word the doctor says. She's acting strange. It makes me nervous when she smiles. Did Mrs. Whittaker take sleeping pills regularly, Doctor?"

"Yes. I suggested she take them," the doctor replied. "She'd been having trouble sleeping."

"Could you take a look at the bottle?" I asked.

I went into the bedroom with the doctor.

"That seems to be about the right number," he said. "She has a fresh bottle every month. Now, Mr. Marley, surely you don't think . . . ?"

"I don't know what to think, Doctor. That's the problem," I said.

"Look, Mr. Marley," Dr. Hughes said, "Mrs. Whittaker was an old lady with a heart problem. Her death is no surprise. Well, there you are, one death certificate. Not much more I can do here. Is someone going to wait here with Martha?"

"I'll do that, Doctor," I said. "And thanks."

I didn't feel I should leave Martha alone with the body. While I was waiting, there was work that Stella could do.

"There's no point in the two of us staying here," I said

to Stella. "Could you go back to the office and call those cab companies? We've got to find Jackie, and soon."

Later, Martha returned with the cookies. She gave me one of her black looks.

"Mmm! My favorite," I said. "When you've made that coffee, come and sit down and tell me all about yourself."

That was pointless. I don't think even Captain Oldenberg would have been successful getting information out of her. The most I got out of her was a simple "Yes," "No," or "Don't know." Anyway, it helped to pass the time while I was waiting for Charlie to turn up. I really wanted to be out on the street looking for Jackie.

Chapter 9 *The lost son found*

Charlie Whittaker arrived at the Century Apartments in the early afternoon. Without intending to, I gave him an unpleasant surprise.

"My God! You frightened the life out of me! So you're Nat Marley?" he said with an amazed look on his face. "You could be my father's ghost. That brings back some bad memories. The way he used to check my homework. He always hit me if I got less than eight out of ten."

"Then I hope appearance is the only thing I share with your father," I said. "I'm sorry about your mother, Mr. Whittaker."

"Thanks," Charlie said sadly, "but we were sort of expecting it."

I sent Martha into the kitchen to make more coffee, and showed Charlie into the bedroom. He pulled back the sheet and stood there looking thoughtfully.

"Well, goodbye Mom," he said finally.

"I know this is not a good time, but could we talk?" I asked. "Wilma Patterson has explained the situation about the will. I wish to say that I never agreed with it. Wilma has my instructions to give everything to the family – money, apartment and so on. I'll just need to sign the papers," I said.

"Thanks. It's not your fault you were caught up in this."

"I'm worried about Martha," I said. "Her behavior's very strange."

"I can't remember a time when her behavior wasn't strange," Charlie said. "You don't have to stay. I can see to everything here now."

"Here's my card. If there's anything I can do, call me."

The Whittaker family had taken up a lot of valuable time. Something we didn't have much of. Back at East 43rd Street, Stella was still calling all the cab companies.

"Oh, hi there. Wonder if you could help me? You don't have a driver named Jackie Clayton working for you, huh? No? Thanks anyway."

She put the phone down.

"Nat," she said, "that makes cab company number fifty. We'll get there eventually."

"Good work, Stella. And if you have to, call Staten Island and Brooklyn too."

Before she could continue, the phone rang. Someone was shouting at the other end. Stella held the phone at arm's length. It was Captain Oldenberg.

"Oldenberg, how are things?" I asked.

"I've been trying to get through to you all morning. Your phone's been busy all the time," Oldenberg replied in his usual direct way. "Thanks for the information about Wiseman. My boys searched his place and you should see the stuff we found there. He's going to jail for a long time."

"Look, Oldenberg, I need to speak to Wiseman."

I explained how we needed to find Jackie Clayton so he could see his dying mother.

"Sure you can speak to him. But will he speak to you?" asked the Captain.

Downtown on the number four express train, I was at Police Plaza quicker than any cab could make it through

Manhattan. Captain Oldenberg was expecting me at Police Headquarters, and took me down to the cells. It brought back memories of my years with the NYPD. Wiseman was his usual sweet self. Physically, he seemed to be in worse shape than Mrs. Whittaker.

"Mr. Wiseman, you remember me? Nat Marley, private investigator. I need your help. I've got to find Jackie Clayton before his mother dies."

"If I could get my hands on him, I'd tear him into little pieces," replied Wiseman.

"Very thoughtful, I'm sure, but that doesn't help me."

"Me and Jackie were partners. Then he left me and broke our agreement. We had an understanding. He won't get anywhere without me. Leave me alone. I don't talk to private eyes. Guys like you make me sick."

At least I'd learned something. Jackie was trying to escape from his past. Maybe when we caught up with him, he'd agree to see his mother. It was now mid-afternoon. I phoned Stella to see how she was doing with the cabs.

"Nat?" she said. "We got something. Patel Cabs on West 14th. I even got to speak to him. But he just said, 'I don't have any ex-girlfriends' and put the phone down."

"This is a job for Joe Blaney," I said. "Get him to watch the place. Can you give me the address?"

"Ninth and 14th," Stella said. "You know, where all the meatpacking places are."

"Right. And tell Joe I'll see him there."

By the time I got there, Joe was already in position. Sitting in his car with his hat pulled down over his eyes, he looked just like a guy sleeping. But I knew he was paying attention to every little movement on that street. Late afternoon. The meat packers had stopped work for the day. We were parked under an old railroad bridge between two huge trucks. Patel Cabs was on the other side of the street a little further up. This could take a long time. We watched and waited. Cabs came and went but no sign of Jackie. As the hours passed, we slowly cooked in the heat. Eventually, I saw him.

"There he is, Joe," I said.

Jackie had changed. This wasn't the hard guy in the newspaper picture. He just looked like any normal guy going about his normal business. I ran across the road and called, "Jackie Clayton! We've got to talk. It's about your mother."

He didn't stop to listen. As soon as I'd said "Jackie," he was running like a frightened man. And he was a lot faster than I was. We lost him in a narrow entrance between two factories. And of course, he knew the area better then we did. Not much more we could do there. Our last chance was to ask at Patel Cabs. The receptionist didn't like the look of us.

"Look," she said to us. "Jackie said if anyone comes around here asking questions, I'm to say nothing."

"Thanks ma'am," I said. "Message understood."

Eight in the evening. I was tired, hot, and hungry.

"Not much more we can do today, Joe."

I made a couple of calls on my cell phone. I told Stella to go home, and asked Dr. Fischer to give Annie a message. If Annie knew we'd seen Jackie, that might just help to keep her holding on to life.

We made our way across to Eighth Avenue. Three blocks uptown there was a Cuban-Chinese restaurant where they did great chicken and rice, and more importantly, ice-cold beer. It made me feel a little better, but I still felt useless.

"Joe, we were so close. Now Jackie will be nervous about any stranger he meets," I said.

"Nothing you could do, boss," said Joe.

"But we've still got one more chance. Oldenberg. We helped him out with Wiseman, so he owes us something. He could give us Jackie's address. The New York Taxi and Limousine Commission holds the records of every cab driver in this city. That information's private, but not to the NYPD."

I phoned Police Headquarters. Fortunately, Oldenberg was still in the building.

"Don't you have a home to go to, Oldenberg?" I asked.

"Marley, I've got teenage kids. Police Headquarters is more peaceful," he laughed.

"I gave you Wiseman so I think you owe me. I need the address of a cab driver. Name of Jackie Clayton. The one I told you about. Drives for Patel Cabs on West 14th. As soon as possible, Oldenberg. His mother's dying."

"I'll do what I can," he said. "But I can't promise anything until tomorrow. The office you need is closed now."

All we could do was wait.

Chapter 10 *We're the good guys*

I hate the way sweat makes your shirt stick to the train seats. I was going through three or four clean shirts a day in this heat. I needed a fresh shirt this morning, but there was no time to change. At the office, Charlie Whittaker and Wilma Patterson were waiting.

"Mr. Marley, thank God you're here!" said Charlie. "I'd like you to come with us to the apartment. I'll explain in the cab. Martha's disappeared."

"OK, let's go. Stella, call me at Century Apartments as soon as Oldenberg calls."

In the cab, Charlie Whittaker explained what had happened. "Mom's been taken to the funeral home. Mrs. Patterson and I agreed to meet at the apartment first thing this morning to start going through mom's papers. I checked into a hotel last night. I didn't like the idea of sleeping in that apartment. We got there at 7:30 AM to find the place in a real mess. There was stuff all over the floor. At first I thought it was a break-in, but Martha's room hadn't been touched. I thought that was strange."

"Is anything missing?" I asked.

"No idea, yet, Mr. Marley. That's where I hoped you would help. Can you find out what's been going on and find Martha? I just feel something is very wrong."

Inside the Whittaker apartment there were books and papers thrown everywhere, broken pieces of furniture and glass on the carpets. The sofas and armchairs had been cut all over and their insides pulled out. The kitchen floor was wet with oil, milk, and wine which was slowly mixing with bags of flour and sugar. A broken bottle of ketchup sat in the bath tub in a pool of shampoo. In the toilet were the torn-up pieces of the Whittakers' wedding photographs.

"Now take a look in Martha's room," said Charlie.

The small, simple bedroom was clean and tidy. There was no suitcase and it looked as if she had taken most of her things. The bookshelf was full of detective stories: Raymond Chandler, Ellery Queen, Ed McBain. On the mirror, she'd written in red lipstick: "Gone to play ball."

"What does the mystery message mean?" asked Wilma.

"I'm not sure yet, but this is definitely Martha's work," I answered.

"What now?" asked Charlie.

"Find everything that hasn't been taken – money, checkbooks, credit cards. We need to find out what's missing. Don't make it look like you've been searching. We shouldn't really touch a thing until the police have been here."

"The police? Do we have to?" asked Charlie.

"Mr. Whittaker, murder is police business."

"Surely you don't think Martha . . ."

"That's exactly what I think. I knew something was wrong all along."

"What do I say?" Charlie asked.

"Report a murder. They'll be here before you put the phone down. And Mr. Whittaker, before you call 911, call the funeral home now. Tell them not to touch your mother's body. If they're preparing it for the funeral, tell them to stop now. The police will have to look closely at your mother's body to find out how she died. There has to be an immediate autopsy."

We had time for a quick look around before the police arrived. No sign of checkbooks, cash, or credit cards. The NYPD team was at the apartment in under ten minutes.

A call came through from Stella.

"Nat? We got an address for Jackie. The Chelsea Arms Hotel. Near the corner of Eighth and 22nd."

"In Chelsea, huh? We went by there last night. This is what to do. Phone the hospital, get a message to Annie. Say we know where Jackie's living. Then see if Jackie's at work. Pretend you're from the Taxi and Limousine Commission. Say you want to speak to Mr. Clayton about a customer who's taken his number and complained about him. That way you should find out when he comes in to work or when he finishes. Call me back here."

Wilma came over with the lieutenant from the Crime-Scene Team.

"We've had a look around, sir," he said. "No sign yet of anything stolen. Mr. Whittaker, can you tell me where your mother kept cash, credit cards, that sort of thing?"

"Her handbag, probably," said Charlie.

The lieutenant turned to one of his men. "Sergeant, did you check that?"

"Nothing, Lieutenant. It was empty."

"Now Mr. Whittaker, do you know where your mother banked?" I asked.

"Chase Manhattan," Charlie answered.

"Would you call them now? We have to know what's happened to her bank account."

As Charlie was about to pick up the phone, it rang.

"It's for you, Mr. Marley," he said.

"Hi, Nat. It's me. I've made the call. Jackie may be at the hotel now," said Stella.

"Has Joe come in? Good. Tell him to wait for me outside the hotel. Now I've got an idea that just might work. Make me up a big, brown paper package. Fill it with old newspapers and magazines and give it to Joe."

"Sure," replied Stella.

Time was very short. I caught a downtown train to 23rd Street. As I came up to street level from the subway, I could see Joe waiting at the corner of Eighth and 22nd, with the package under his arm. He was pretending to read the *Daily News*.

The Chelsea Arms Hotel had seen better days. Now it just looked like any other cheap hotel. The floor was dirty white stone in the lobby. A guy was working on the computer, behind the window at the reception desk. There was another big guy sitting at a table opposite the reception desk. He was obviously there in case of any trouble.

"Joe, stay just outside the door on the street. Keep an eye out. If Jackie tries to run, stop him any way you can."

Now, I hoped this was going to work. I quickly wrote a message on the package and wandered over to reception.

"Is there a Mr. Jackie Clayton staying here?" I asked. "Package for him."

"You can leave it with me," said the receptionist.

"Sorry. Special package," I said. "Has to be signed for by Mr. Clayton."

"I'll call the room."

A minute later Jackie came down the stairs into the

lobby, looking nervously from side to side. I waved the package at him.

"What's this?" he said. "I'm not expecting anything."

"Read it," I said. "It's for you."

Jackie took the package. The message read: "Jackie – your mother is dying and wants to see you. Time is short."

He wasn't sure what to do. I moved around to cut off the stairs. Jackie threw the package in my face and made a run for the front door, only to see Joe standing in his way. Then he tried to hit Joe. Not a good idea. Especially when the guy you're trying to hit is an ex-NYPD heavyweight boxer. Joe replied with his famous straight left. A loud cry of pain from Jackie. He fell backwards into my arms.

The big guy at the table stood up. "Stop that or I'll call 911!" he shouted.

I held my license in his face.

"Nathan Marley, private investigator," I said. "I've been hired by this guy's mother to find him." I turned to Jackie. "Listen, Jackie, your mom's seriously ill. We're the good guys. We're not from Wiseman. Your mother hired us to find you. You've got to believe us. Look, get reception to call Bellevue Hospital – then you'll believe us."

Jackie was calming down. He nodded to the guy at reception who called the hospital and then passed the phone to Jackie. Jackie spoke slowly and quietly. "Do you have a patient there by the name of Annie Clayton? . . . You do? . . . I'll be right over." Jackie put the phone down, turned around, and took our hands. "Guys," he said, "I owe you an apology. I thought you were more unwelcome guests. Let's move. I haven't seen my mom in twenty years."

Chapter 11 *Martha Bianchi*

The hospital was more or less directly east across town. A cab was the best idea and we found one on Eighth Avenue.

"Driver, Bellevue Hospital," I said.

On the way, I told Jackie his mother's story.

"So mom's been on the street all this time?" he asked.

"Ever since she last saw you – in a cell," I said.

"I thought I knew everything," he said. "Thought I was hard and tough and didn't need anybody. Now I know better. Families are part of you. I used to think Wiseman and the boys were family. But they weren't any more family than the driver here. As long as you were doing your job OK, it was cool. But one mistake and you were out."

"What was your mistake, Jackie?" I asked.

"I wanted a normal life. I was tired of looking over my shoulder for cops. I wanted an ordinary job and a place I could call my own. Then I started thinking of my family. Hey, are we going to be in time?"

"We'll make it OK," I replied.

"Wiseman hates it when people try to leave the organization," Jackie continued. "The last twelve months I've been trying to earn a living and hide from him at the same time. It was almost impossible to do both. I tried to find mom and went back to the Bronx, where I grew up. Everything's changed. Didn't even recognize my own street.

All the old housing projects pulled down. Nobody had heard of Annie Clayton."

We stopped outside the hospital. The driver had earned his twenty-dollar tip. The clerk at reception phoned Dr. Fischer, who came down immediately to meet Jackie.

"Jackie Clayton, the long lost son. You're going to make your mother a very happy woman," she said.

"How is she, doctor?" asked Jackie.

"To be honest, she doesn't have long to live. She hasn't got the strength. All those years on the street. But she's holding on for you. Take it easy when you go in. She gets tired very easily. We'll go right up," said the doctor.

Jackie turned to me. "Nat, will you come in with me?"

"Sure," I said.

Annie was asleep, her mouth open. The doctor shook her arm gently. "Annie, he's come back," said the doctor.

The tiredness disappeared from her face. A wide smile. Tears in her eyes. Jackie took her hand.

"Why! If it isn't my big stupid son come back to see his mom after all these years," she whispered.

"Sorry, Mom. I was a no-good kid. I've changed. I've been trying to find you."

"Come here. Let me hold you tight. That's better."

"Mom, this guy Nat's amazing. He didn't give up."

Annie turned to me and smiled. Underneath the smile, she was exhausted.

"Nat, I don't know how to thank you," she said softly.

They needed to be alone together. My day wasn't finished, though. I called Stella at East 43rd Street.

"Nat, how's it going?" she asked.

"We found Jackie," I said. "Joe persuaded him to listen.

He's with Annie now. The doctor doesn't expect her to live much longer."

"Poor woman," Stella said.

"Stella, you've done more than enough for one week. You found Jackie. Close the office and enjoy your weekend. I'm going back to the Whittaker apartment with Joe."

I wouldn't have minded a weekend off myself. The effects of the heat and tiredness were beginning to hit me. There was a line of cabs outside the hospital. Joe and I jumped in the first one.

The traffic was heavy, but the delay gave me time to think. What was in Mrs. Whittaker's bedtime drink? Could the autopsy establish it was the drink that killed Mrs. Whittaker? If Martha had the strength to destroy furniture, she would easily be able to murder Mrs. Whittaker. But how? She appeared to have died peacefully and the doctor didn't seem to think there was anything unusual about the death. The cab was now standing still in the traffic. An opportunity to get some sleep.

Joe shook me awake at the Century Apartments. In the apartment, the Crime-Scene Team was getting ready to leave. Charlie Whittaker and Wilma Patterson were checking through papers. Some were wet and dirty. I didn't want to think what Martha had poured over them.

"Any news from the funeral home?" I asked the lieutenant.

"We were lucky, sir," he said. "They hadn't prepared Mrs. Whittaker for the funeral and there'll be an autopsy this evening. Not much more we can do here."

Charlie Whittaker turned to me. "Guess what," he said. "The lieutenant interviewed all the neighbors. They all heard some noise during the night, when Martha destroyed the furniture. They thought it was a wild party. Since when did my mother have wild parties?"

"Would have been some party," I laughed.

"There's nothing wrong with the locks," Charlie went on. "No break-in. It all looks like Martha's work, Mr. Marley. Most of my mother's papers are here. Ugh! There's ketchup on this one. But no checkbook or credit cards. I phoned the bank and luckily there was someone there who could help. I had to go over there myself. The bank account's overdrawn. It looks like Martha's taken out tens of thousands of dollars."

"Spending it on what, I wonder," I said.

"Mr. Marley, find that woman, and quick," Charlie said. "I want her to pay for what she's done."

"We're on the job, Mr. Whittaker. First, we need to go through everything in Martha's room."

The message "Gone to play ball" was still on the mirror.

"What sort of 'ball' might that be, boss?" asked Joe.

"Was Martha a baseball fan?" I asked. "The answer's got to be in here somewhere. We can start by going through these books."

There was a shelf full of old detective stories which looked as if they had been read again and again. That only told us she liked reading. Then Joe found a book open on the floor by the bed.

"Look at this book, boss," Joe said. "Martha's been marking parts of it."

The book was called *The Perfect Murder*. The pages were yellow with age.

I looked through the book, reading what Martha had underlined. One sentence especially caught my eye:

"She kicked a bit when I put the pillow over her face. But it was soon all over. If killing is so easy, why not do it again? They say 'practice makes perfect.'"

I showed it to Joe.

"I think Martha reads too much," he said. Joe pointed at the inside cover of another book. "Look. She's been practicing how to sign Mrs. Whittaker's name."

I showed the book to Charlie Whittaker.

"Is this how your mother signs her name?" I asked.

"That's it. That's how Martha managed to get the money out of mom's bank account."

We went back to our work in Martha's room. No suitcase, no handbag. Her own things were missing. We then started on the pile of vacation booklets that Joe had found under the bed. Las Vegas, Oneida, and Atlantic City.

"There's only one sort of ball you can play at these places," I said to Joe. "And that's in a casino."

Martha could now be losing all Mrs. Whittaker's money at a casino. We didn't know where she had gone and there was no way we could phone a casino and ask, "Do you have anyone at the gambling tables matching the following description . . . ?" Even if a casino did agree to help, there could be any number of middle-aged women losing their money. The type of people who save up all year for a week's gambling vacation. They spend every cent and go home poor.

"Where do you think she's gone?" I asked Joe.

"My guess is nearer rather than further," he replied.

"Atlantic City is the closest," I said. "Do you know how many casinos there are in Atlantic City? At least ten, maybe more."

There was hardly anything in the room that told you Martha had a life of her own. We had searched everywhere for a photo of her. Nothing to show to people. Our only course of action was to visit each casino until we found her.

"So what now, boss?" asked Joe.

"Atlantic City's several hours' drive away," I said. "We may need to spend all day there. Bring your car to the office, nine o'clock tomorrow. And make sure you get some rest."

I paused for a moment. I'd just had a thought.

"Joe, isn't this all a bit too obvious? If Martha really wanted to disappear, why write that message and leave the books? Somehow, I think she wants us to find her. As if she's acting out one of those detective stories. But who knows?"

It seemed to be hotter than ever. I'd had enough. When was this weather going to break? It was going to be another long day tomorrow and I'd lost my weekend. I had some bedtime reading to do – *The Perfect Murder.*

Chapter 12 *Atlantic City*

I had stayed awake reading most of the night. Not by choice – I just couldn't sleep in the heat. At sunrise I gave up and got dressed. Outside it was almost pleasant. That wouldn't last long. There was time to stop by Bellevue Hospital. I knew it would be too early to visit Annie, but maybe the nurse would be able to tell me the latest on Annie's condition.

At the hospital, the nurse took me to the door of Annie's room and raised her finger to her lips.

"Not a sound," she whispered. "Just look at this."

Annie Clayton and her son Jackie were both asleep. Jackie was sitting beside the bed with his head on the pillow. Annie's hand was in Jackie's.

"He hasn't left her all this time," said the nurse.

"What about Annie?" I asked.

She led me away from the room. She looked serious. I was expecting the worst.

"There's nothing more we can do," the nurse said. "It's just a question of waiting. It could be today or tomorrow."

"I'm sorry," I said. "Call me if there are any developments."

At East 43rd Street, I called Police Headquarters to check if there were any results from the autopsy on Mrs. Whittaker. The news didn't make me feel any better.

"They say she died of a heart attack. If it's a natural death, then there's nothing more to do."

"What about the results of the drug tests?" I asked.

"It's too early. Tomorrow, maybe."

The problem was how to make the NYPD believe it was murder. If the drug tests showed there was a normal level of the drug in her body, we couldn't show that Martha murdered her – unless she admitted it.

Joe arrived at the office bright and fresh. Me, I couldn't stop yawning.

"Why are you so cheerful?" I asked him on the way to his car.

"I got a good night's sleep, boss, just like you suggested," Joe replied.

"Well, I'm exhausted. Wake me up in Atlantic City."

I stretched out on the back seat and soon fell asleep. The best sleep I'd had for days. Several hours later, Joe woke me as we were entering the city, along the Atlantic City Expressway.

"You've been sleeping like a baby, boss," he said.

Unlike the city, the casinos were beautiful buildings in every possible design and color. We parked and walked along beside the ocean, and started looking inside the casinos. It was the same story in each one. Lonely people kissing goodbye to good money. But no sign of Martha. We had visited five casinos by the time we arrived at the Golden Palace.

"I don't believe it, boss!" Joe said. "I've never seen anything like it."

On our way in, we passed a line of large, white stone elephants. Inside it was a dream world. The lights above were clouds of brilliant stars. Soft music was playing. Dark wood, deep carpets, shining gold and silver everywhere.

Early afternoon, and people were crowded around the roulette tables.

"Over there, Joe! It's Martha."

There she was, sitting between two old ladies. Martha made them look tiny. In front of her, Martha had piles of brightly colored casino chips. She was playing for big money and had placed chips on numbers 7, 14, 21, and 28. The ball shot around and around and finally landed on 7. Martha screamed with laughter.

"It's me again!" she shouted. "That's the way to do it. I knew I couldn't lose!"

I couldn't watch her any longer. I went up to her.

"Martha," I said. "We've got to talk."

"Well, if it isn't Mister Private Eye himself," she answered. "I wondered when you'd get here. Leave me alone. I'm winning."

She started placing more chips on the table. That was enough. I pushed them onto the floor.

"Hey, what do you think you're doing?" she shouted.

"Excuse me," said a voice behind me. "Is there a problem here?" There was a heavy hand on my shoulder. I turned around. A tall, powerful guy in a black suit, wearing his casino ID on his jacket.

"Leave this lady alone and get out before I call the police," he said.

I held up my investigator's license. Now I had to move fast. Everything depended on Martha admitting to murder.

"Nat Marley, private investigator," I said. "This lady is using stolen money. Money she stole from her employer, who she murdered. Didn't you, Martha? We know everything about the money and the pills. Just like it said in that detective story you like so much."

There was total silence around the roulette table. People stared at us with open mouths. I held up Martha's book.

"Aren't you the clever one!" said Martha. "I was wondering how long it would take you. Faster than I expected. Sure I got the idea from the book. Couple of extra sleeping pills in her hot chocolate. Then it was no more 'Martha do this, Martha do that!' Just put a pillow over her head. She kicked a bit, but it was all over in seconds. Easy. And her face looked perfect. Everything happened just like the book said it would. Only quicker and easier. It was her own fault. She left me out of the will!"

"You read too much," I said.

The man in the suit was beginning to understand.

"You'd better come to the office," he said. "Do you want to call the police, Mr. Marley?"

"With pleasure," I said. "And would you collect all those chips. That's stolen money."

It was another couple of hours before we were finished at the Atlantic City Police Headquarters. Martha admitted everything again to the New Jersey police. She wasn't sorry at all. In fact, she seemed to be enjoying it.

"What now, Lieutenant?" Martha asked. "You going to lock me up in a cell?"

"Yes. Until the NYPD comes to get you," the lieutenant replied. "Sergeant, take her away. Now, Mr. Marley, I'll speak to Captain Oldenberg. This is NYPD business."

It was late afternoon. We had to get back to New York. I could make some calls on the way. I'd been thinking about

Annie all day. I managed to get through to Dr. Fischer at Bellevue. She didn't expect Annie to last the night and Jackie had been asking for me. There was no time to lose.

Another call, to Charlie Whittaker who was waiting to hear from us. Luckily, he was still at the Century Apartments.

"Mr. Whittaker?" I said. "We found Martha. In Atlantic City."

"You did? She murdered my mother?" asked Charlie.

"She admitted everything," I told him. "It was just like I thought. She was gambling at the casino like she was a millionaire."

"The money's not important," Charlie said. "I want her to pay for what she's done."

"Don't worry. She will."

It was dark by the time we reached the hospital. Jackie was waiting for us outside Annie's room.

"You guys are great, all you've done for us," said Jackie.

"Don't mention it. How's Annie?" I asked.

"Mom's going slowly. She's unconscious now. She managed to talk about old times. At least she's not in pain."

"We'll stay with you, Jackie. At a time like this you need friends around you. I've known your mother for a long time. I want to be there when she leaves us."

Jackie went back inside. We waited until early morning, watching the hands of the clock move around and around. A hospital is a very strange place at that time of night. The dying waiting, hour after hour, for the moment of death. At 2:30 AM, the nurse called Dr. Fischer. After a quick examination, she waved to us to come in. Annie's breathing was now slow and irregular. Finally, it came to a stop. Jackie was still holding his mother's hand.

"I'm sorry, Jackie. She's gone," the doctor said.

Jackie looked up at us. "She never gave up hope for me," he said. "Could you leave me alone with mom for a minute?"

Outside, Joe looked at me closely.

"Nat! You've got tears in your eyes," he said.

"Tears? Me? No, must have got something in my eye."

He was right though. Annie's death had affected me deeply. More than I had imagined it would. But I hadn't felt a thing when Mrs. Whittaker died. Ten minutes later, Jackie came out.

"Let's get you home, Jackie," I said sadly. "I'm going to miss those morning chats with Annie at Grand Central."

Chapter 13 *Rain*

Another Monday morning. When I walked out of Grand Central to 42nd Street, the sky was heavy with black storm clouds. You could almost feel the electricity in the air. At last the weather was going to change. As I got to the office, fat raindrops were starting to hit the sidewalk.

Stella was at her desk as usual.

"Nat, there's a visitor," she said.

"Who?" I asked.

"Go and see."

"Why the mystery?"

The sky was suddenly lit up. Then darkness and a crash of thunder. Inside the office was a face I knew only too well. Another crash of thunder. Pouring rain. The storm had started.

"Oldenberg! You sure know how to frighten a guy."

"I love this, Marley," Oldenberg said. "Did you know there's always less crime during bad weather?"

"You're not here to talk about the weather. Why *are* you here?"

Oldenberg wanted to speak to Jackie Clayton. He needed his help to put Wiseman in jail. In return, the police had promised Jackie a new life with a clean record. Jackie trusted me so I was asked to set up the meeting.

After Oldenberg left, the storm got worse. Rivers of rainwater in the streets. And more visitors. Stella showed in two workmen.

überrascht

"Nat, a pleasant surprise this time," Stella said.

"Mr. Marley, we've come to put in the air conditioning," said one of the workmen.

"I don't believe it. Why weren't you here last week?" I asked.

The crashes and bangs as they started putting in the units made it almost impossible to work. Maybe I should move somewhere with a better climate. Like Alaska. Who needs air conditioning in Anchorage? It wasn't the best time to get another visitor. It was Wilma Patterson. She wanted me to arrange a meeting with Jackie at her office tomorrow morning to read his mother's will. Then the phone rang. More crashing and banging from the workmen.

"Can you guys stop that for just a minute?" I asked. "Marley here. Sorry about that."

"It's Charlie Whittaker. I need your advice. I've been speaking to Captain Oldenberg. The police aren't sure if Martha can be tried for murder."

"Go on," I said.

"There's no problem with the money," Charlie said. "The checkbook and credit cards were in her handbag. She definitely stole it all. But as for murder. The woman's crazy. She seems to be living in a dream world of detective stories. No one can say if she's telling the truth or telling another story. The autopsy results don't help us either. Nothing definite from the results of the drug test so it's still a natural death. What do you advise, Nat?"

"She'll go to jail for a long time for stealing the money and what she did to the apartment," I said. "She knew exactly what she was doing when she emptied your mother's bank account. It's a difficult one, Mr. Whittaker. It looks as if she'll be tried for stealing, not murder. But either way, she'll be in jail for a long time. And life in a New York State jail is no picnic. I'd accept what Oldenberg says. You know and I know she's guilty of murder. But getting people to believe it is another matter."

"Well, that's not what I wanted to hear," said Charlie. "But I don't suppose there's much we can do about it now. Anway, if she isn't tried for murder, they can return mom's body sooner for the funeral."

Another call. This time it was Jackie, to tell me that Annie's funeral was going to be at 11:00 AM on Saturday morning in Queens. I promised to be there. Jackie said he could make it to Wilma's office at ten o'clock tomorrow to hear his mother's will. I wasn't sure how he was going to take Oldenberg's suggestion.

"One more thing, Jackie," I said. "I know it's not a good time, but Captain Oldenberg wants to see you."

"I don't like the sound of this, Nat," Jackie said.

"Just hold on, Jackie. They want to get Wiseman, but they need dates, times, names, places, and so on. In return, they'll forget about anything you might have done for Wiseman in the past. This could be the fresh start you need."

"That's a lot to think about, Nat," Jackie said. "I'll tell you tomorrow."

With all the noise in the office it was impossible to work. "We're going to take a long lunch break," I shouted to the workmen. "There are the keys. If you finish before we're back, leave them in the lobby. If those units don't work . . ."

"Trust us, mister," said one of the workmen. "We could do this in our sleep."

The long lunch break lasted most of the afternoon. I was feeling increasingly tired after all the action last week. I left Stella to lock up the office and escaped back to Queens to get some sleep.

The next morning, midtown Manhattan smelled fresh and clean after the storms. A cloudless blue sky. Was it going to be another hot one? Then I remembered. I'd paid seven hundred dollars for air conditioning. Those units had better work. As I stepped inside the office at East 43rd Street, I could feel ice in the air.

"What's this?" I asked. "Siberia?"

"Sorry, Nat," said Stella. "Just having a little trouble with the air conditioning."

"Well, I'd rather fry than freeze."

"Come on, Nat! I'm doing my best. I can't always be right. I'm just a human being, not superwoman. Oh, by the way, Wilma Patterson phoned. Could you be at her office by nine thirty?"

At Wilma's office, there was a pile of papers for me to sign. Everything that Mrs. Whittaker had left to me would now go to Charlie Whittaker and his sister Betty Osborne, in equal shares. Just the way it should have happened in the first place.

"Nat, there's the question of your fee," said Wilma.

"I'll get Stella to send Mr. Whittaker my bill," I said.

"That won't be necessary," she said. "He told me to give you this. He hopes it's enough." She handed me an envelope full of money.

It was more than enough. Very kind. Now I wouldn't

feel so bad about the air conditioning. By ten o'clock, Jackie, Wilma, Stella, and I were sitting around Annie's metal box. Wilma took the key and unlocked it.

"Mr. Clayton," she said, "your mother's will is very simple. Everything in this box is yours to use as you wish."

Inside was a pile of papers. On top lay an envelope with the words "For my son, Jackie." Jackie opened it and read the letter aloud.

"To my darling son, Jackie,

I don't know where you are but I've been keeping this for you all these years. A present from the daddy you never knew. He was a big businessman. If what's here is worth anything, use it to give yourself a future.

Your loving mom

All that time she remembered me," said Jackie. "But what are all these papers? And what does this note mean?"

Wilma took the papers and note from Jackie and looked through them.

"Mr. Clayton, this note must be from your father. Listen:

Annie – I can never be a real father to the child. Here's some money to help with food and clothes. And something for the future. Keep these stock certificates. One day they might be worth a lot of money.

Yours,
Tom"

"Who's this Tom?" asked Jackie.

"The answer must be here somewhere," said Wilma. She

searched through the papers until she found the stock certificates. "Your mother has taken good care of you. See these certificates? This stock could be worth tens of thousands. Everything's been done properly. The stock is in your mother's name and they were given to her by . . . I don't believe it: Tom Whittaker!"

"What's going on?" asked Jackie.

"Jackie, I think I know who your father was. I remember Annie telling me she had once worked as an office cleaner, where she met the top man in the company. That man was Tom Whittaker. A big businessman, president of Whittaker Air."

In my wallet, I still had the photocopy of the *Daily News* story with Tom Whittaker's picture.

"That's him, Jackie. Keep it. And that's not all, Jackie. You've got family. A half-brother and half-sister. Charlie Whittaker and Betty Osborne. They live upstate."

Jackie was silent for a while, then he turned to Wilma.

"Mrs. Patterson, there's something I have to know. It's important. What would have happened if mom had died without seeing me? Or I had refused to see her, or if Nat never found me, or if I had died. If, if, if . . ."

"Just in case anything like that happened, Annie added an extra part to the will," Wilma explained. "The money from the sale of the stock would have gone to help homeless women. I don't think Annie had any real idea of its value."

"Mrs. Patterson, could you keep the stock certificates here for me?" Jackie asked. "I need time to think."

There were more things in the box. Some black and white family photographs. A young mother with a happy, smiling baby in her arms. Class photographs from an elementary school. Childhood birthday parties. Family days out on Coney Island. Now they were in color. An active, young teenager holding a baseball bat. Jackie's eyes were shining as he looked through the photos. The poor guy had gone through so much in the last few days. Lost his mother and found a family. A guy with no future now had hope. We sat in silence as Jackie discovered his childhood again. A few minutes later he was ready to speak. Now, he looked calm and confident.

"Nat, Mrs. Patterson," Jackie began. "My mind is made up. Mrs. Patterson, will you find out what this stock is worth? There's mom's hospital bills to pay, and Nat needs to be paid for all his work."

"Certainly," said Wilma.

"And Nat. You said I've got a half-brother and half-sister. I'd really like to meet them. They're family. You know the Whittakers, so would you arrange a meeting. And one more thing. I've been thinking about what you said yesterday. The answer's 'Yes.' I've got to do it if I want to make a clean break from my past. Call Captain Oldenberg. I'll do anything he wants if it's going to get Wiseman off my back and in a prison cell."

"Leave it to me, Jackie. We'll see you at the funeral."

Chapter 14 *The Annie Clayton Center*

There were no more than ten people at Annie's funeral, including Annie's friends Ellie and Leona, and Charlie Whittaker and Betty Osborne. I introduced Jackie to Charlie and Betty. They were still talking together when I left.

Mrs. Whittaker had a grand funeral a day or so later in Albany, with family and a few old drinking partners of Tom Whittaker. I had gone because I thought I should, not out of choice. The surprise was again seeing Jackie Clayton with Charlie and Betty. Maybe he had found his family.

Life had been quieter since mid-July. I had even taken a vacation. After that, I just got on with the usual daily work – divorce or looking for missing persons. Nothing exciting, but I wasn't complaining. I preferred it that way. Toward the end of September a letter arrived from a New York State prison. It was from Martha, but it looked like a child's handwriting.

To Mr. Nat Marley, the Private Eye,

I've had more fun in the last two months than I've had in the last twenty years. I like it fine here in jail. Everyone looks after me. Makes for a change. Nice people. I get along real well with my cellmate. She's inside for murder.

Martha

So Martha enjoyed life in jail. Life behind bars must suit

her character. With her size and strength, she probably wouldn't get any trouble from the other prisoners. From her letter it sounded like they were good to her – better than Mrs. Whittaker had ever been. Anyway, society was safe from Martha Bianchi.

At last the heat of the summer was over, and I was enjoying my favorite season, fall. The trees in Central Park had turned into a sea of red and gold. Life in the office continued as normal. Fall turned into winter. In the office, Stella complained as much about the cold as she had about the heat the summer before. We were both glad when spring arrived.

It was one morning in spring that I found a surprise invitation in my mail. It was for the opening of the Annie Clayton Center on 125th Street. Stella and I could hardly believe it. So Jackie had found a way to give his mom something back after all.

On the morning of the opening, Stella, Joe and I traveled uptown to Harlem together. Outside the Center was a group of important-looking people. Community leaders and local politicians. Reporters from newspapers and local TV stations. At the front door stood Jackie Clayton, Charlie Whittaker, and Betty Osborne.

Charlie Whittaker spoke first.

"Ladies and Gentleman, I'd like to welcome you to the opening of the Annie Clayton Center. A building that will provide comfortable rooms for the homeless women of this city. Everyone will be welcome, no matter what her color or religion. The women who use this center will have one thing in common – nowhere to live. My sister and I, and my half-brother Jackie Clayton have all lost mothers recently. This building is in their memory."

Then Jackie stepped forward. He had changed since I had seen him last. This wasn't the frightened cab driver I had met in July. He looked and sounded confident as he spoke.

"Thank you, Charlie. My mother, Annie Clayton, lived on the streets of this city for over twenty years. She needed love and care, and as a young man, I refused her that love and care. If there had been a center like this, perhaps she could have been saved from the city streets. I sincerely hope that this center will provide for women like my mother for many years to come."

Charlie and Betty then joined Jackie. Betty spoke.

"Finally, we'd all like to say a special thank you to the man whose hard work made this all possible. Without him, we might never have met. An old friend of Annie Clayton's – Mr. Nat Marley."

She pointed toward me. Television cameras turned at the same time. Interviews with reporters followed. I had my photograph taken with Jackie and the Whittakers for the newspapers. It would be a great human interest story. Finally we were able to escape. Jackie took us into an office.

"We all owe you and your partners a big thank you for all you've done," said Jackie. "After the funerals, Charlie, Betty, and I got to talking and found we had a lot in common."

"Strange. The Bronx meets the Upper West Side," I said.

"You see, we've all lost mothers. And in different ways, we've had difficult childhoods. I was always getting into trouble on the street," said Jackie.

"And we had a cold, unloving father," said Charlie. "I

still remember what it felt like growing up in that apartment. The things he used to do to mom."

"It was when I met Ellie and Leona, mom's old friends, that I started thinking," said Jackie. "Some way of using mom's money to help people like them. I talked it over with Charlie and Betty."

"The apartment was ours, but after everything that had happened, we never wanted to set foot in there again," said Charlie. "I felt we had to do something. Jackie's idea was to put our money together to do something to help improve people's lives. It's been a lot of hard work, but all worth it."

"What more can I say? This place is a great achievement," I said. "Annie was right never to lose hope in you, Jackie."

Finally we said our goodbyes. I started thinking as we walked along 125th Street in the sunshine. I'd said before that I'd seen the best and worst of life in this city. I was wrong. This Center was the best I had ever seen. I still had mixed feelings, though. Annie had lived on the streets of New York while she'd had enough money for a place to live. She'd suffered when she didn't have to.

Stella touched my hand.

"You feeling all right, Nat?" she asked.

"Just thinking. The Annie Clayton Center. Something to remember her by. Almost like she has life after death. If only she'd known the value of that stock. She could have enjoyed life before death."

"She never had her fair share of what life can offer. But others will, Nat, others will."